Personal Follow-up
Leader's Manual

MATTHIAS MEDIA
Sydney • London • Cape Town

Personal Follow-up Leaders Manual (2nd Edition)
© Matthias Media, 1996

St Matthias Press Ltd. (A.C.N. 067 558 365)
PO Box 225
KINGSFORD NSW 2032
AUSTRALIA
Ph: (02) 663 1478 Fax: (02) 662 4289

St Matthias Press (UK)
PO Box 665
LONDON SW20 8RU
ENGLAND
Ph: (081) 947 5686 Fax: (081) 944 7091

St Matthias Press (SA)
27 Auburn St
Denneburg
Paarl 7646
SOUTH AFRICA
Ph & fax: (21) 872 2560

Scripture taken from the HOLY BIBLE, NEW INTERNATIONAL VERSION. Copyright © 1973, 1978, 1984 International Bible Society. Used by permission of Zondervan Publishers.

ISBN 1 875245 49 9

All rights reserved. Except as may be permitted by the Copyright Act, no part of this publication may be reproduced in any form or by any means without prior permission from the publisher.

This edition of the Personal Follow-up Training Course is based on the 3rd Edition of *Just for Starters* (ISBN 1 875245 50 2).

Cover design by Wendy Potts

Contents

Introduction for Leaders 5

Leaders's Notes for...

Unit 1 9
    1.1   Introduction to the course
    1.2   What is Follow-up?
    1.3   Who is Responsible?
    1.4   Assignment

Unit 2 13
    2.1   The Importance of Follow-up
    2.2   Getting Started in Follow-up
    2.3   Introduction to *Just for Starters*
    2.4   Preparation for Meetings
    2.5   Assignment

Unit 3 17
    3.1   Essentials for Follow-up
    3.2   Discuss Meeting 1
    3.3   Assignment

Unit 4 21
    4.1   Goals for Initial Follow-up
    4.2   Discuss Meeting 2
    4.3   Assignment

Unit 5 25
    5.1   Personal Qualities for Follow-up (1)
    5.2   Discuss Meeting 3
    5.3   Assignment

Unit 6 29
    6.1   Personal Qualities for Follow-up (2)
    6.2   Discuss Meeting 4
    6.3   Assignment

Unit 7		 33
7.1	Developing Relationships in Follow-up	
7.2	Discuss Meeting 5	
7.3	Assignment	

Unit 8		 35
8.1	Overcoming Problems	
8.2	Discuss Meeting 6	
8.3	Assignment	

Unit 9		 37
9.1	Continuing in Follow-up	
9.2	Review Questions	
9.3	Discuss Meeting 7	

Introduction for Leaders

Welcome to *Personal Follow-up*, a course for teaching Christians how to follow up new or young believers and establish them in the faith. Specifically, the course aims to equip Christians with the knowledge and skills to be able to develop a strong relationship with a new or immature believer and take them through the fundamentals of Christianity using the *Just For Starters* series of Bible Studies.

Because it equips Christians to help and serve others, *Personal Follow-up* has tremendous potential for strengthening our churches and fellowships. *Personal Follow-up* can mobilize a task force of more mature Christians in your fellowship to nurture their younger brothers and sisters. Trainees learn the basic principles of helping other Christians to grow, and in particular how to use a set of basic Bible studies as a framework for doing this. What church would not benefit from having a team of well-equipped disciplers who could establish lasting relationships to encourage new or immature believers?

Nor is it a difficult course. Many churches have found *Personal Follow-up* to be ideal as the first basic piece of training they encourage their members to undertake as they reach the stage of being stable, mature Christians.

This course, and the *Just for Starters* set of Bible studies which accompanies it, has been around in various forms since 1979. Since that time it has been used to train thousands of Christians in the skills of personal follow-up. In this third edition, we have smoothed out a few wrinkles, revised some details in line with changes to *Just for Starters*, and given the whole course something of a face-lift.

About this manual

This Manual contains Leader's Notes for all the sessions in the *Personal Follow-up Trainee Workbook*. You'll find information about the goals for each section and key points to be communicated, as well as additional discussion questions, tips on how long each section should take, and miscellaneous tips on running the course.

This introduction contains general adivce on how you, as the leader, can prepare for each session and run the course most effectively. Before reading on, **skip over to Unit 1** and refresh your memory about the goals and content of the course.

How to prepare

The quality of your training will be reflected in how well young believers are followed up. This should be sufficient motivation to do your job thoroughly!

Part of your responsibility will be to make sure that each trainee:

- has correct understanding of, and answers for, the *Just For Starters* studies
- does careful preparation for each meeting
- completes all of the Strand 1 work to help their understanding of follow-up
- commences follow-up with someone (if possible).

The only pre-requisite for you personally is to have used the *Just For Starters* studies in personal follow-up. It is hard to train someone else in the realities of follow-up if you've never done it. If you have followed up (or 'discipled') a young Christian, but haven't used the *Just For Starters* studies, start doing the studies with a new or young Christian before you start teaching the course. It is important that you are familiar with the studies and able to answer questions about their content and direction.

Before each meeting with your trainees:

- Pray for them and for the session you are preparing.
- Do your own thinking about the passages or discussion questions.
- Refer to the *Leader's Notes* for comments and suggestions.
- Write up your notes and answers in your own copy of the *Trainee Workbook*, including how long you plan to take for each section, any supplementary questions you'd like to ask and so on. (NB. When writing in your timing, it's a good idea to record it as the time past the hour so that you can see at a glance how you're progressing).
- When leading the Group, don't refer to this *Leader's Manual*. Have everything you need written up in your *Trainee Workbook*.

Writing up your notes not only helps you to prepare more thoroughly, but improves your relationship with the group. You are a leader who has done the work and thought about it, not someone who is simply reading somebody else's answers out of a book.

Practical Training

Following up a new or young Christian is a practical skill, and it is hard to master a practical skill in the classroom. You learn practical skills by practising them. It is important, therefore, to encourage your trainees to actually *do* some personal follow-up.

Aim to have all your trainees involved in following someone up by the beginning of Unit 4. It might be someone who has recently become a Christian, or someone in your church or Christian group who is young in the faith and would benefit from doing the studies. Don't make it a matter of law, but emphasise the benefits of learning by doing. By starting at around Unit 4, they should remain 'in front'— that is, have discussed the studies in the group before doing them with the new Christian.

What You Will Need

To be able to run the course you will need the following:

- Trainee Workbooks and *Just For Starters* studies for yourself and each of the people you are training.
- This Leader's Manual for yourself.
- A copy of L.J. Crabb's book, *Encouragement*.

Beginning Each Training Unit

You need to work out how to begin each unit. There is nothing set down, and what you do will depend on your trainees, the time available, and so on. Here are a couple of suggestions:

- Prayer
    - for each other (you might use the 1 Thessalonians 1-3 studies to find things to pray about)
    - for each other's ministries
    - for individuals we are following up or helping in some way
    - for church/campus ministry

- Review previous work (you could prepare review questions on material that you thought needed revising).

unit 1

Before doing anything else, make sure everybody in the group knows each other.

Work out some way to start building rapport within the group. Get to know each other (if you don't already) by having people share information about themselves—e.g. how they were converted; what Christian book has been the most help to them and why; who is their 'hero'. Alternatively, use some other 'getting to know you' exercise—eg. break into pairs and talk about yourself for one minute; the other person then introduces you to the group.

Pray.

Time
10 minutes

1.1 Introduction to the Course

Read through the 'Introduction to the Course' notes together to give an overview of the Course. Elaborate and answer any questions.

Goals (for this section)

- To help the trainees have motivating expectations of what will be accomplished by the training.
- To set norms for the group—e.g. personal involvement, commitment to learning together, sharing difficulties and joys, working hard at doing the course and the assignments.

Emphasise that there is quite a lot of homework, but that there is much personal encouragement and challenge to our own lives as we do the Bible studies and prepare to teach others.

Recommend that they read Crabb's book, *Encouragement,* during the training.

Time
10 minutes

1.2 What is Follow-up?

Have the trainees write their definitions in their workbook. Then have people read out their definitions and draw together the common threads.

Key Points

You should come up with something like: Establishing a new believer in the faith. Share Colossians 2:6,7 with them. Strengthen in the faith = make fast, fix, confirm, consolidate, establish. This is the essence of follow-up: establishing lasting foundations in the faith.

Time
10 minutes

1.3 Who is Responsible?

Have the trainees write answers by themselves and discuss them as a group.

Goals

- To reach a balanced view of responsibility for personal follow-up:
    - we are responsible to care for each other
    - yet, it is God who gives the growth
    - and there is a point at which the individual is responsible for his own spiritual state.

    (Ultimately, we can't 'blame' ourselves if someone we are following up rejects our efforts, or back-slides)

Key points

1. 1 Thessalonians 5:23 etc

   God.

   ADDITIONAL QUESTION:
   "WHAT DOES GOD USE IN OUR LIVES TO BRING US TO MATURITY?"
   Circumstances/trials (James 1:2-4)
   Scriptures (2 Timothy 3:16,17)

2. Hebrews 10:24 etc

   Fellow believers and ministers.

   ADDITIONAL QUESTION:
   "WHAT CAN WE DO TO HELP THE GROWTH OF OTHER BELIEVERS?"
   Pray for them and each other (Philippians 1:9-11)
   Meet with them to encourage them (Hebrews 10:24,25)
   Meet with each other for mutual encouragement
   Teach each other the word of Christ (Colossians 3:16)

3. Jude 20 etc.

   The believer himself.

   ADDITIONAL QUESTION:
   "WHAT CAN THE BELIEVER DO TO GROW IN CHRIST?"
   Obey Christ as Lord
   Read, understand and apply the Bible
   Pray
   Be in regular fellowship with other believers

Time
10 minutes personal study
15 minutes group discussion

1.4 Assignment

Stress the importance of doing these assignments. They are essential for the discussion in Unit 2.

2. If the trainees do not already have their copies of *Just for Starters,* you will need to hand them out here. Even though the introduction to the studies is in Unit 2, encourage them to have a go at the first study now.

Time
5 minutes

unit 2

2.1 The Importance of Personal Follow-up

Discuss this section, compiling a list of the major points.

Goals

- To provide further motivation for being involved in personal follow-up
- To stress the advantages of working with individuals

Key Points

- *It allows for individual needs to be met (a person can more easily hide real needs in a group).*
- *It allows careful teaching and application of the Bible.*
- *It guards against the vulnerability of the new Christian to doubt or discouragement.*
- *It allows for personal relationship and for the new believer to be listened to and understood.*
- *It exposes the new believer to the life of a more mature believer.*
- *The new believer can learn to follow-up another new believer.*

ADDITIONAL QUESTION:
"ARE THERE ANY ADVANTAGES OVER GROUP FOLLOW-UP"?

Time
10 minutes

2.2 Getting Started in Follow-up

Read through the notes in the workbook together and answer any questions.

Goal

- To lay the groundwork for encouraging each trainee to get started in follow-up; i.e. to start doing *Just for Starters* with someone.

Time
15 minutes

2.3 Introduction to *Just For Starters*

Read through the notes together.
Outline the content of the seven studies showing how they fit together progressively.

Goals

- To show that the studies are a good framework in which to do personal follow-up
- To show that one of the key advantages of *Just for Starters* is that it teaches good Bible reading habits
- To explain how they are used

Key Points

Outline of contents of *Just for Starters*

#1 & #2
The Gospel, Salvation
Knowing that I am a Christian

#3
Obedience, the conflict, how salvation by God's grace is reflected in a changed life.
How do I live now?

#4 & #5
The Bible, Prayer
How do I relate to God now?

#6
Meeting with other Christians
How do other Christians help?

#7
Concern for the salvation of others
How do I relate to my non-Christian friends?

Make sure you actually show the trainees how to do this type of study, as an example of how they themselves will show a new believer. Do the first two pages of Study 1 together, emphasising the points listed in the Workbook under 'How To Do the Just For Starters Studies'.

Explain that it is best to do part of the first study with a new Christian to show how the study should be done. The subsequent studies can be done privately and then discussed in your meetings together.

Time
15 minutes

2.4 Preparing for Meetings

Read through the notes together, referring to Appendix A. Do some of the preparation for Meeting 1 together to give them the idea.

Time
15 minutes

2.5 Assignment

3. In line with what the group has looked at in this unit, introduce the idea of them actually doing some follow-up with a new or younger Christian—starting soon. Emphasise the advantages of practicing what they are learning while they are learning. At the same time, don't make it into a law. Some of the trainees may not be able to find someone. It is a little early for them to actually start doing the

studies with someone, but it is not too early to be praying and thinking about who they might start with in the next few weeks.

Time
5 minutes

unit 3

3.1 Essentials for Follow-up

Discuss their thoughts from 1 Thessalonians 1-3 together, with the group adding to their notes from the discussion.

As extra preparation for yourself, you could read Acts 17:1-10, 13-15 re. the circumstances surrounding the conversion of the Thessalonians.

Key Points:

- *Rely on God to establish people*
    - *faithful in prayer and thankfulness (1:2,3)*
    - *example of prayer (3:10-13)*
    - *not simply with words, but with power, with the Holy Spirit and with deep conviction (1:5)*
    - *God at work (2:13)*

    Compare 1 Corinthians 3:5-7 and 1 Thessalonians 5:23,24

- *Expose new believers to the Bible*
    - *our Gospel came to you (1:5)*
    - *the word of God at work in you who believe (2:13)*

- *Aim for life changes, not superficial response*
    - *faith, love, hope (1:3)*
    - *work, labour, endurance (1:3)*
    - *turned from idols to serve the true God (1:9)*
    - *urging you to live lives worthy of God (2:12)*

- *Godly life of the helper*
    - *you know how we lived among you for your sake (1:5)*
    - *you became imitators of us and of the Lord (1:6)*
    - *you are witnesses...how holy, righteous...we were among you (2:10)*
    - *integrity and motives crucial (2:3-5)*

- *Love for the new believer*
  - *strong opposition faced (2:2)*
  - *motivated by love to share life as well as the Gospel (2:8)*
  - *mother/child relationship (2:7)*
  - *father/child relationship (2:11)*
  - *intense longing (2:17)*
  - *you are our glory and our joy (2:19,20)*

Time
25 minutes

3.2 Discuss Meeting 1

Discuss *Just For Starters* #1. Ensure that each trainee understands the passage and study. This is a key aspect of the training course. It is most important that the trainees have a solid grasp of the passages, so that they can answer any questions that the new believer might have (the accompanying tape series is a helpful aid in this—see the back pages of the *Trainee Workbook*). To be able to teach a passage of Scripture to someone else—even a short passage like this—requires a thorough understanding of the content and the context. You should also make sure that the trainees themselves understand the gospel—this would be a basic qualification for doing follow-up.

Some suggestions on how to conduct this session (and following sessions where the Meetings are discussed):

- Consider breaking into smaller groups of 2-4. For this first discussion, it may be better to all stay together.
- Discuss each other's answers to the *Just For Starters* study, including the additional verses. Trainees can swap studies with each other to stimulate thinking.
- Trainees share their 'main points' and 'additional goals' for the meeting.
- For Meeting 1, emphasise that this first study is important for determining where people are 'at'. Especially in public evangelism, some who 'make decisions' are not yet converted. This should become evident through the first *Just For Starters* study. Often the first step in following someone up is to go through the gospel clearly.
- Give individual help to any trainees who cannot explain the gospel clearly

(perhaps teach them the *2 Ways to Live* method of personal evangelism). The first two studies ('Saved by God' & 'Trusting in God') are helpful in leading someone to faith and repentance.

Goals

- To stimulate each other's thinking on how to handle each study and meeting
- For the trainer to evaluate the quality of preparation
- For the trainer to ensure high quality preparation

Key Points

For each of the Meetings in the following units, we will list some key aspects of the study. These notes are meant to give you some idea of the thinking behind the seven studies, and the key truths that they seek to express. These notes should be helpful in compiling your 'main points' for each meeting.

Saved by God

- The logic of the passage is that our future salvation is the assured outworking of our present justification and reconciliation (N.B. the use of 'now' and 'future' in Questions 4-6).
- Question 7, therefore, is the key question in this study, because it highlights the central idea of the passage: we can be sure that we *will* be saved because we are *already* justified.
- Many Christians (not so much the new, untaught Christians as those doing the follow-up) have difficulty with the study because of two errors:
  a) They do not distinguish between justification and salvation. In the New Testament, salvation is sometimes talked about as having happened in the past; at other times it is spoken of in the present. In this passage it is *future*. It is being rescued from God's wrath on the Day of Judgement. Justification is our present state, which we enjoy because of Christ's death on our behalf.
  b) Their assurance for the future is based on their own efforts rather than on God's justifying work in Christ. They think they have assurance of salvation because of their faith or repentance or good works or feelings.
- The basis of our assurance is not our subjective response to God but his objective work on our behalf in the cross of Jesus.
- This first study takes you to the heart of the gospel. It often sorts out whether

or not the person you are following up is a Christian.

Time
30 minutes

3.3 Assignment

3. Encourage the trainees to try to initiate a follow-up relationship this week. Pray about it together, asking God to provide opportunities. Begin Unit 4 by finding out how it went!

Time
5 minutes

unit 4

Before starting the Unit, talk and pray about part 3 of their assignment—to ask someone to do *Just for Starters* with them. How did it go?

4.1 Goals for Initial Follow-up

Read Ephesians 4:7-16 together and discuss answers from the Assignment.

Goals

- To show that the goal of follow-up is for the new believer to grow to maturity in Christ and, ultimately, to be involved in serving others
- To show that the ministry of follow-up is consistent with Biblical teaching about ministry

Key points

1. What is the goal of Christian service?

   For the body of Christ to be built:
   - *the church to be built or completed*
   - *by individual Christians being built-up*

   Christians are to be built up in:
   - understanding
     - unity in the faith, knowledge of the Son (v. 13)
     - stability in doctrine, resisting wrong teaching (v. 14)
     - speaking the truth (v. 15)
   - godliness
     - maturity to the measure of Christ (v. 13)
     - speaking the truth in love (v. 15)
     - the body builds itself up in love (v. 16)

ADDITIONAL QUESTION:
"IN WHAT WAYS SHOULD THE BODY OF CHRIST BE BUILT UP?"

By being built up in understanding and godliness, Christians grow up into Christ, the Head (v. 15).

2. What goals should we have in follow-up?

Building up the new believer
- *established in the truth of the gospel*
- *life changed by the gospel*
- *his or her ministry to others*

Some specific goals:
- *Ensuring that the new believer has a clear understanding of the gospel and is certain of his or her own salvation*
- *To teach the new believer some fundamentals of Christian living*
- *To teach the new believer to be concerned for others*

3. What changes would begin to be seen in the life of someone who had these goals?

- *Experiencing certainty of salvation based on the work of Christ; working to change his or her life and to overcome sin*
- *Understanding and accepting the teaching of the Bible*
- *Concern for others*
- *Willing to be identified as a Christian*

Time
25 minutes

4.2 Discuss Meeting 2

Key Points

Trusting in God
- This study is not about future salvation but salvation that has already taken effect ("you *have been* saved").

- The emphasis of the passage (and the study) is God's gracious activity, rather than our efforts to save ourselves.
- Even my response to the gospel ('faith') is nothing I can boast about—my whole salvation is a gift from God.
- The constant emphasis in the study of God alone/grace alone is meant to help people grasp the meaning of faith. Faith is resigning oneself to God; it is not the 'thing' I have to do, the good work which saves me. Faith looks not to its subject ('my faith') but to its object ('faith in God').
- Some have found this study repetitive—the same right answer keeps recurring. However, the study is aiming to drive home a point that young Christians *must* grasp: that God saves us; we do not save ourselves.

Time
30 minutes

4.3 Assignment

Encourage the trainees to find someone to follow up if they have not already done so.

Time
5 minutes

Personal Follow-up

unit 5

5.1 Personal Qualities for Follow-Up (I)

Consistent Life

Discuss your answers to the 1 Thessalonians 1-3 assignment. Other references to look at are:
   1 Timothy 4:11,12
   2 Timothy 3:10f.
   2 Thessalonians 3:7-9

Goal

- To stress the importance of the example and quality of our own Christian lives as we follow up a new or younger believer

Key Points

1. What verses show the importance of the *life* of the person doing follow-up? What did Paul say about his life and his co-workers?

1:5	*The Thessalonians knew how Paul and his friends lived—they lived for the sake of the Thessalonians.*
1:6-7	*The Thessalonians imitated Paul and his companions and the Lord. The Macedonians and Achaians in turn followed the Thessalonians.*
2:3-5	*Pure motives and integrity.*
2:10	*The Thessalonians witnessed their lives—holy, righteous, blameless.*
3:5	*They were passionately concerned for the Thessalonians.*

2. Why is our personal example of godliness important?

    - *To avoid hypocrisy.*
    - *Our teaching and life must be consistent.*
    - *See Matthew 7:3-5 on the hypocrisy of correcting another before oneself.*

- *The power of example.*
- *The new Christian must see the gospel lived out in us. They will tend to imitate us.*

3. What implications do you see for yourself?

- *Must examine our own godliness and seek to please God.*
- *New believers must see Christ in us, and the deeper the relationship the more they will see. We must be open, honest, and transparent with the new believer to reduce the gap between image and identity. As Crabb would put it, we need to 'peel off our layers'.*
- *We become vulnerable—it is threatening to let someone else see our lives. We must have our security in God's acceptance of us.*

Time
25 minutes

5.2 Discuss Meeting 3

Key Points

Living God's way

- The first two studies emphasise the work of God in our salvation, that we contribute nothing, and that our first and basic response is trust/faith. This third study concentrates on a second aspect of our response—the changed life that results from what God has done for us in Christ.
- God's grace didn't save us so that we would continue to live as we did before. His purpose in Christ, as it says in the verses following our passage, was to "redeem us from all wickedness and to purify for himself a people that are his very own, eager to do what is good" (Tit 2:14). And so his grace teaches us to do just this: to say 'No' to worldly desires, and to live a godly life.
- It is important to get this in the right order and to understand clearly how God's salvation and our good works fit together. The grace comes first to save us, and then teaches us to lead a changed life. We are justified, forgiven and cleansed *so that* we might lead a new life, not the other way round.
- The struggle to say 'No' to the world and to live God's way takes place while we are 'waiting'. It takes place in an attitude of expectation, as we look ahead

to the blessed hope of Jesus' second appearing. This ties in with study 1. Our Christian lives are framed by two momentous realities—the justification/reconciliation that has already taken place through Christ's death, and the final salvation or reappearing of Christ that is yet to come. And so our good works both look backwards to what God has already done (his grace for salvation) and they look forward to what lies ahead (the blessed hope).

- The *Other parts of the Bible to look at* section draws attention to the role of the Holy Spirit in all this. To say that God's Spirit leads us to put to death the 'misdeeds of the body' (Rom 8:13) is really another way of saying that God's grace teaches us to say no to ungodliness. God is at work in us, urging and leading and enabling us to live his way. This is what it means to be 'led by the Spirit' (cf. Gal 5:18, the only other place where the phrase 'led by the Spirit' is used in the New Testament).

Time
30 minutes

5.3 Assignment

Questionnaire

Do the Questionnaire as an assignment for next week. You may need to provide help if personal problems arise in the Questionnaire. Stress that the answers won't be discussed in the group and that the idea is to think honestly about our own lives before God.

Time
5 minutes

unit 6

6.1 Personal Qualities for Follow-Up (2)

Genuine Love

Get the group to skim back over 1 Thessalonians 1-3 and answer questions 1-3. Do this individually. (They should be starting to get familiar with these chapters!) Discuss their answers together. Then move on to answer questions 4-6 in the group. Perhaps have different group members look up the references in question 5.

Goals

- To focus on a particularly important aspect of our godliness towards the person we are following up: love.
- To emphasize that follow-up isn't a calculating, impersonal operation. It is all about loving the other person (and whatever preparation and planning we do should only spring from that).

Key Points

1. Skim back over 1 Thessalonians 1-3 and list out the evidence of Paul's love for the Thessalonians.

1:2	*always thanking God for them*
1:3	*continually remembering them before God*
2:2	*faced strong opposition*
2:7	*avoided financial burden*
	gentle like mother with her child
2:8	*shared their lives as well as the gospel*
2:9	*worked, toiled and endured hardship in order to avoid financial burden*
2:11	*father and child relationship*
2:12	*encouraged, comforted, urged them*
2:17	*intense longing to see them*
2:19,20	*they were his glory and joy*
3:2	*sent Timothy to strengthen, encourage*

> 3:5   *afraid their faith might have been sabotaged (passionate concern)*
> 3:7,8   *encouraged because of their faith*
>   *Paul really lived knowing that they stood firm*
> 3:10   *prayed earnestly, night and day to see and help them*

2. Why is this aspect of follow-up important?

- *Follow-up means caring for a person and their relationship with God, not going through a process.*
- *Follow-up is often difficult and if we are not committed to the person we will quit.*

3. How does Paul illustrate the relationship he had with the Thessalonians? What phrases particularly highlight it?

> 2:7-12   *Family commitment*
>   *like a mother caring for her children*
>   *as a father deals with his children*

4. What are some of the aspects of the parent/child relationship that are relevant to us as we help someone grow in Christ?

- *Need for relationship.*
- *Sensitivity and understanding.*
- *Meeting individual needs.*
- *Belief in the worth of every individual.*
- *Follow-up is not a formula, a syllabus or using some method.*
- *We must catch the heart of it: love, involvement, value of each person.*
- *We must get involved in their lives—we can't go through the motions of follow-up in a detached, impersonal, mechanical way.*

In the discussion, draw out the personal sacrifices which Paul and his companions made in order to help the Thessalonians.

> 1:2,3   *they gave time and energy to prayer*
> 2:2   *they faced physical persecution, possible imprisonment and death (Acts 17:1-9)*
> 2:9   *physical labour*
> 2:17   *cost of time etc. to see them*
> 3:5,7,8   *his concern for them affected his well-being*

ADDITIONAL QUESTION:
"WHAT ARE THE PARTICULAR ASPECTS OF THE PARENT/CHILD RELATIONSHIP TO WHICH PAUL REFERS?"
- *The dependency of the child on the mother, not vice versa*
- *The example, encouragement and urging by the father*

Ask questions to elaborate what these attitudes will mean in practical terms.

5. Consider the examples of Jesus, John, Paul and Epaphras in these passages. What attitudes should you have towards those you follow-up?

Mark 10:45	*serve them, give up your life for them*
John 15:12,13	*lay down your life for them*
3 John 4	*committed to their walking in the truth*
Galatians 4:19	*agonizing over their growth in Christ*
Colossians 4:12,13	*wrestling in prayer, working hard for their maturity*

Time
30 minutes

6.2 Discuss Meeting 4

Key Points

Listening to God
- While it may seem obvious that the point of this study is the inspiration and authority of the Scriptures, the importance of these doctrines lies in their consequence, i.e., the sufficiency of the Scriptures.
- Thus, Question 3 (and the Think it Through immediately preceding it) are important. We listen to God only where he speaks to us, in the Scriptures; and we are saved only through the gospel which the Scriptures contain.
- If the young Christian can grasp the idea that we need nothing more than the Bible, he will be safeguarded from all manner of heresies and false teachers.
- The overall aim is to have the new believer 'doing the word of God'. The study does this indirectly by helping the Christian to see the reason for submitting to the Bible as the sole authority in life.

Time
25 minutes

6.3 Assignment

Time
5 minutes

unit 7

NB. There is a little less material in this unit than in the others. Use any extra time you might have to catch up on unfinished work from previous units or to pray together.

7.1 Developing Relationships in Follow-up

Lead a discussion using these questions. Trainees should write notes during the discussion.

Goals

- To start to think practically about how to develop a loving, personal relationship with someone you are following up

Key Points

2. There are many practical things we do in relating to our friends. List some of these that will help us care for the new believer and get to know them.

> *Some examples:*
> - *Have meals together*
> - *Visit his or her family*
> - *Invite him or her to your home and your circle of friends*
> - *Play sport or do something else enjoyable together*
> - *Watch your dress and manners (keep them appropriate)*
> - *Don't only talk about superficial things; share about family, background, likes/ dislikes, etc.*
> - *Phone regularly just to say hello*
> - *Write notes*
> - *Do 'necessities' together (shopping etc.)*
> - *Show special kindness when sick, under pressure etc.*

Time
20 minutes

7.2 Discuss Meeting 5

Key Points

Talking to God
- It is important that the new believer be introduced to relating to God in prayer.
- This requires a right attitude to God, who welcomes us to make our requests of him on all matters. Because God is concerned for us, and because nothing is too big or too small for his attention, we can address our prayers to him, with thanksgiving.
- However, we must also teach the young Christian that praying is not the same as 'getting'. The Sovereign Father may decide that other things are better for us than those for which we ask. But whether we receive what we ask for or not, prayer is always profitable because it keeps us in relationship with God. The worries and anxieties that lead to prayer can be dealt with, even though we may not receive what we asked for (in the terms in which we asked).
- Correct teaching on God's promises about prayer at the start of our Christian life can spare us many anxious hours and false paths later in our pilgrimage.
- Many Christians are confused over this passage, having been taught that we will receive a sense of 'peace' in prayer when we ask for the right thing, or when God has guided us. Note carefully what the sentence actually says: "the peace of God … will guard your hearts and minds in Christ Jesus."

Time
30 minutes

7.3 Assignment

Time
5 minutes

unit 8

8.1 Overcoming Problems

Lead the discussion. Trainees should write notes during the discussion.

Goals

- To allay some of the fears trainees might have about potential problems in follow-up
- To prepare trainees to meet potential problems—forewarned is forearmed
- To deal with any actual problems that have arisen in the follow-up that the trainees are already doing

Key Points

List some of the problems you envisage may arise in a follow-up situation; ie. attitudes or circumstances that may hinder growth.

Discuss possible ways of dealing with these difficulties, looking at why they arise and the Bible's attitude towards them.

- *Unwillingness to do the Just For Starters Studies or receive any kind of structural help.*
  - *Work out the reason for this, explain the value of structured study, and be flexible. Do whatever they will do in Bible study which will help them grow.*
- *Many decisions are not conversions.*
  - *Be alert to discern this and explain the gospel clearly.*
- *Questions about the Bible's authority.*
  - *What is the motivation of the question: intellectual problems or avoiding obedience? Deal with accordingly.*
- *Difficulty in building relationship.*
  - *Be patient—we can't force friendship.*
  - *Meet other Christians as well.*
  - *Adjust to his concerns and interests.*

Time
25 minutes

8.2 Discuss Meeting 6

Key Points

Meeting with God's family
- People hold a wide variety of views about church-going. Many of these ideas undermine the gospel and need to be counteracted in the thinking of the new Christian.
- One of the chief errors is that we somehow get right with God by offering him worship in church. Another wrong idea is that the Church is an authoritative institution full of rules and regulations.
- The study emphasizes gathering together for the mutual ministry of encouraging one another to obey the word of God. This is the essence of 'church'. The questions are designed to reflect the passage's exhortation for us to encourage one another to live by the gospel in the light of the day of Christ.

Time
30 minutes

8.3 Assignment

Stress the importance of having all preparation completed, especially an accurate understanding of the Study passages. Reassure the trainees that the Review Questions are not a test—they won't 'fail'. They are a guide for the trainees to help them evaluate how much they have learnt.

Time
5 minutes

unit 9

9.1 Continuing in Follow-Up

Lead the trainees in this discussion.

Goals

- To ensure that follow-up is an on-going process, not just a once off 'hit' with seven Bible studies

Key Points

1. How can we make sure that the new believer receives continued help?

    - *We keep providing individual help.*
    - *We arrange for others to help by getting them into a church.*
    - *Both of the above. Often this is best, since we can care for them personally while they benefit from the church ministry.*

2. What can we do on a one-to-one basis to continue help?

    - *Pray for/with them. Teach them to have a life of prayer.*
    - *Study the Bible together.*
    - *Read chapters or books of the Bible together and discuss.*
    - *Follow Bible reading programmes with questions, e.g. Search the Scriptures (IVP), or the Interactive Bible Studies series from Matthias Media.*
    - *Study and discuss their questions and problems.*
    - *Do ministry together to help them learn, e.g. evangelism (embark on the Personal Evangelism course).*
    - *Continue to 'socialise' together, enjoying each other's friendship.*

3. How would you help a new believer choose and relate to a church?

- *Teaching of the church.*
  Minimum requirements:
  - *full divinity of Jesus (1 John 4:1-3)*
  - *authority of the Word of God, as delivered by the apostles (1 John 4:4-6)*
  - *justification by faith alone (Galatians 1:6-10)*
- *A church where they can be built up and help others.*
- *Go with them, meet the minister and talk with him about how the new believer can relate to the church.*
- *Keep contact at least during the transition into church to sort out any difficulties.*

Time
15 minutes

9.2 Review Questions

Briefly run through the answers to these together. Suggest that they go back over any material that they hadn't grasped.

Goals

- The aim here is not to test the trainees to see if they have 'passed', but for them to become aware of what they have (and haven't) learnt.
- To bring together the threads of Strand 1 of the course

Time
5 minutes

9.3 Discuss Meeting 7

Key Points

Meeting the world

- One of God's great concerns is the salvation of his people. To this end he did not spare his own Son. Part of the new believer's growth in godliness will be

- a concern for the salvation of others. (Note how the *Other parts of the Bible to look at* section drives this home.)
- This passage in Colossians envisages evangelism taking place on two levels. There are those Evangelists like the Apostle Paul, whose job it is to proclaim the message. And it is the responsibility and joy of all us to support them, encourage them and pray for them, that they should proclaim the message clearly. At another level, all of us interact with 'outsiders' each day. By the wisdom of our lives, and the nature of our speech, all of us should also make the most of opportunities that come our way, and be ready to answer anyone.
- In other words, all of us may not be Evangelists (capital 'E'), but stemming from our concern for the salvation of others, all of us will be supporting evangelism, and all of us will be engaged in it on a personal level as we have opportunity.
- Note the importance both of wise, consistent Christian living and gracious, salty speech. Both are necessary.
- Our conversation with outsiders has two characteristics: it is gracious (easy on the ear, kind, sensitive, etc.); and it is 'seasoned with salt' (challenging, interesting, not insipid). Much interpretative effort has gone into nailing down precisely what 'seasoned with salt' signifies—whether it is an allusion to Old Testament covenant rituals involving salt, and so on. It is most likely, in context, that it is simply a counterbalance to graciousness. Our conversation is to be kind and generous, but not completely lacking in flavour. This kind but sparky manner of speaking is how we should answer outsiders, as we talk to them about the gospel.
- This study can lead to a consideration of how to evangelize, and so to some form of training (such as the *Personal Evangelism* course).

Time
20 minutes

Terminating the Group

You will need to allow sufficient time for the conclusion to be as productive as the other parts of the Course. One of the important things you will need to consider is how you—the trainer—will 'follow up' your trainees over the next few months. It is important that you model the concern and persistence that is so much a part of personal follow-up. You might arrange to meet each of them individually to see whether they have been able to use the skills they have learnt and whether they have potential to train others in follow-up.

What to do to round off Session 9:

1. Evaluation

Briefly discuss what the group set out to achieve by doing the course.
Talk about what has/hasn't been achieved and why. Discuss any criticisms of the way the course was structured. Ask the group to share the benefits they have received from the training.

2. Continuing in Follow-up

Realise the loss of support of the group—no homework tasks or encouragement in follow-up.
Go over what motivates us to do follow-up and whose work it really is.

Suggestions for continuing in follow-up:
- Start following up a new believer as soon as possible if you haven't started already.
- Use the *Just For Starters* studies in contexts other than follow-up. Share with another Christian, small group, Sunday School, houseparty, etc.
- Ways of continuing to encourage each other even though the group is ending:
   - prayer list or prayer partners for a month
   - meet with someone to discuss and pray for the person you are following up

3. Prayer Time

Pray for your work in follow-up and for individual prayer requests.

Time
20 minutes